OUR

SAUCE

THE MISSING INGREDIENT TO YOUR PRAYERS

J.B. ARMSTRONG

Instagram | Twitter: _jbarmstrong

www.jbarmstrongfilm.com

Our Secret Sauce: The Missing Ingredient To Your Prayers

www.advisedbyamber.com

Cover illustration by Isaiah Rose
Email: sonofjhovah@gmail.com
Instagram & Twitter: irose_art

Printed in the United States of America

ISBN-13: 978-0-578-85044-3

DEDICATION

Mom - Thank you for teaching me the value of vision. You remind of what true sacrifice looks like. With every dream that I had, you made it your mission to nurture it to fruition, with a passion for my personal growth and mental development.

Dad - Thank you providing me with the value of life. You remind me that Jesus is the way and the truth and life itself. Your commitment to faith and the testimony of God's unwavering mercy is the foundation of my spiritual DNA. Thank you for your guidance.

Paw Paw - Thank you for providing me with the gift of wholeness. Your creative essence lives on. Your wise council and sound mind still captives my heart to this day. May you always have a reason to smile when you look down on me.

Bishop Hugh Daniel Smith, Jr. - Thank you for your spiritual instruction. Your mentorship and leadership has shaped my understanding of God and the work of His Son in ways that have truly changed my life.

FOREWORD

"... I have come that they might have life, and that they might have it more abundantly."

-St. John 10:10 (KJV)

What's significant to note in this passage of Holy scripture is that Jesus used the word ***might*** when referring to possessing an abundant life. Most humans I meet are talking about or are on the quest to make their lives better. They're endeavoring to reach a quality of life that they've dreamed about since they were children. I believe Jesus said ***might*** because there would be some work required of all of us to realize this "abundant life" that He was speaking of.

Jesus isn't a magician. He doesn't just make everything you want appear out of thin air because you asked for it. He requires that you mix the faith you have in Him with the personal work necessary to receive all of Him (James 2:17). Simply said, you have to do "the work."

I liken this point to a person who gets a new job. They apply, land an interview, and are eventually hired in. In most cases before this new employee gets the reward of a paycheck, they will have to first do the work the job requires for a at least a couple of weeks. He or she agrees to do the work with the faith and belief that come Friday, direct deposit should be on its way. Had they not fulfilled necessary work required, having an expectation for compensation would be foolish. This is why the Lord said ***might***, because having an expectation for an abundant life without having done the work, which is ***prayer***, is in fact foolish.

J.B. is one of the reasons why I don't have to do the work alone. As life would have it, we've experienced joys and triumphs, heartbreaks, and unforgettable milestones together. He and I have known each other for over ten years. We became friends, then best friends, and now I have the privilege to call him a true brother. We both found ourselves in a space where we were seeking to figure out our lives, while trying to please God in the process.

God has allowed our friendship to be a cemented cornerstone that we can go to for prayer, guidance, and when needed, intervention. While seeking the "abundant life" our friendship has been a proven source for encouragement, correction, and joy.

As a young man with big dreams, I wanted everything to come at the time I planned for it; house, marriage, kids, six-figures, etc. I had God on my time schedule. Of course, the Lord doesn't work like that, but being naive led me to believe that God would grant all of my dreams and visions simply because I had faith that He could. And He could because He's God... but like any good relationship, communication is essential and prayer should be your daily communication with God.

The abundant life that we want exist on the other side of the work that we really don't want to do. If possible, we would take every shortcut and detour to get to where we think our destination ought to be. But if you don't do the necessary work while enduring sometimes painful circumstances, your destination will not mean as much to you. It won't be as sweet as it should be.

In *Our Secret Sauce: The Missing Ingredient To Your Prayers*, J.B. instructs us to remember that the shortcut and detour that most of us are trying to avoid is "the work!" He posits that a healthy prayer life and a pure heart before God makes it possible for us reach our abundant lives. He lays out a proven recipe that has provided an overflow of grace in his life and mine. *Our Secret Sauce* is not just a book for you to read. It's a book for you to apply right away. It needs to be a staple in your home, never to collect dust on your bookshelf, but to be used as a handy tool to aid you in doing the work toward getting to and sustaining an abundant life.

- Minister Orlando P. Bailey

THE INTRODUCTION

Prayer is the ultimate cheat code to unlocking the grandeur of God's abundance within our own lives. Philippians 4:6-7 (NLT) tell us:

6 *Don't worry about anything; instead, pray about everything. Tell God what you need, and thank Him for all He has done.* ***7*** *Then you will experience God's peace, which exceeds anything we can understand. His peace will guard your hearts and minds as you live in Christ Jesus.*

As believers, it is imperative that we model ourselves after the man that Jesus was while he was here on this physical earth. Once we begin to examine Jesus' existence outside of the prophetic gift and atonement of sin that He was (and still is today), we can then really begin to comprehend the existence of Jesus as simply a man.

He was a spiritual being having a natural experience. From this, it is safe to assume that Jesus wrestled and fought against the same tests and tribulations that we encounter daily while searching for evolution and growth in God. It is my objective and aim to cover three essential biblical points to help better illustrate what the posture of proper prayer should look like based on the life of Jesus.

Jesus Prays in Gethsemane

Mark 14:32-38 (NLT)

32 *They went to the olive grove called Gethsemane, and Jesus said,*
"Sit here while I go and pray." ***33*** *He took Peter, James, and John with*
him, and he became deeply troubled and distressed. 34 He told them,
"My soul is crushed with grief to the point of death. Stay here and keep
watch with me."

35 *He went on a little farther and fell to the ground. He prayed that, if*
it were possible, the awful hour awaiting him might pass him by. ***36***
"Abba, Father," he cried out, "everything is possible for You. Please take
this cup of suffering away from me. Yet I want Your will to be done, not
mine."

37 *Then he returned and found the disciples asleep. He said to Peter,*
"Simon, are you asleep? Couldn't you watch with me even one hour? ***38***
Keep watch and pray so that you will not give in to temptation. For the
spirit is willing, but the body is weak."

This entire passage alone is a revelation to the foreseeable relationship that believers were to have with the one true God. This experience–this exchange–was the blueprint for a much larger framework for prayer. There was no magic wand. No rubbing of lamps or charging of crystals, but a simple petition. Jesus' ***faith*** was in His ***Father*** whom He knew had all things worked out to fulfill one of the greatest sacrifices ever.

Three things stand out here: (1) the men in Jesus' company during this particular voyage, (2) where they were going, and (3) the emotional state of mind Jesus was in at this particular time. Let's take a look.

The Four cardinal Gospels (Matthew, Mark, Luke, and John) all detail this critical moment in the life of Jesus from, at times, vastly different perspectives. Prior to this walk that Jesus takes with His disciples, was one of the most notorious dinner parties that ever took place: The Last Supper. It's during this last meal with some of his most beloved friends and followers that Jesus proclaims the coming glory of the Father, the salvation of humanity, and His ascension into Heaven to take His rightful place next to God. He even details and foreshadows his own betrayal; the plot to kill him and who will even do it. *Imagine that.*

Imagine not only knowing the good that your death would do for the world, but also imagine experiencing the hurt of *knowing* someone would willingly betray you, thus leading to your death. Or what about having the perspective and insight to know that a trusted friend, who stood by your side for years, who–when the time comes–will deny that they even knew you.

Let's pause here earnestly for a moment. Picture the kind of weight that would be on your shoulders. You are dying, yet you know you have a purpose; a purpose that is much larger than death itself. Your friends and family seem to support your dreams and ideas, but they gossip behind your back about the very thing you are believing God for. Or what happens when God has given you revelation on how all things will work out for your good, but it will take 20 years for the vision to manifest properly in your life? What. Do. You. Do?

Jesus knows the hour that is at hand and decides to leave their place of communion to do the only thing He can do when hard pressed by life's circumstances. From the small house they were all huddled in, hours before His death, Jesus and His disciples begin traveling to a small garden called Gethsemane not too far from town. Now, it is important to quickly note that Gethsemane's literal translation means "oil-press," but we'll get to that a bit later. Track with me.

Throughout the entire New Testament, Jesus and His disciples frequent this small garden tucked away on the backside of The Mount of Olives. This should suggest that (A) Jesus was going to a familiar place; a place where He knew he could find the presence of God, and that (B) it was secluded. It was away from everything that was against Him. It was away from the Upper City and its religious ideals. It was away from the judicial law. It was away from those who were sick and broken. It was away from the literal world that needed saving. Jesus had to physically distance himself from anything that could be a distraction in order to serve His purpose and vision.

Now, it's my belief that Jesus was initially on His way to seek His Father for what could be considered a casual encounter. A check-in of sorts. I mean, this is the virgin-conceived Son of Man. He knew the entire game plan from front to back. He had all of the answers for what was to be done and expected by God. He even possessed miracle-working powers, so I can't imagine Him needing more than just a few minutes to make sure things were going according to the plan He *already* knew. But, the Bible tells us something interesting in Mark 14:33-34 (NLT):

33 *He took Peter, James, and John with him, and he became deeply troubled and distressed.* **34** *He told them, "My soul is crushed with grief to the point of death. Stay here and keep watch with me."*

I don't think there's ever a more revealing time of Jesus' vulnerability and human experience than this one. The Lion of Judah's ***soul*** was crushed with grief…to the point of ***death.*** The first verse alone signifies, that prior to this point, Jesus was what could be classified as "fine." He *became* deeply troubled and distressed. Life reached a point in His life where He found himself feeling as if He was dying. He felt as if he couldn't take life anymore, and the burdens of His circumstances began to cause him distress.

The Oxford Dictionary defines distress as extreme anxiety, sorrow, and pain. Don't these feelings sound like the same issues and internal conflicts we sometimes find ourselves battling? When a loved one dies unexpectedly? Or when the promotion you needed in order to adequately cover new bills falls through? Or when you find out that the love of your life has been cheating the entire time you were together? Or when the plan you set for your future doesn't line up to the will of God and you find yourself turning to substances for healing? How do you combat your grief and your sorrow?

Jesus reflects each and every one of us during this moment in the garden. He was struggling with His purpose and felt like everything was over–like he could literally die from the turmoil he faced physically. But look at how He responds to His own personal distress. Mark 14:35-36 (NLT) reads:

35 *He went on a little farther and fell to the ground. He prayed that, if it were possible, the awful hour awaiting him might pass him by.* **36** *"Abba, Father," he cried out, "everything is possible for you. Please take this cup of suffering away from me. Yet I want your will to be done, not mine."*

Matthew 26:39 (NLT) says it another way: **39** *He went on a little farther and bowed with his face to the ground, praying, "My Father! If it is possible, let this cup of suffering be taken away from me. Yet I want your will to be done, not mine."*

Luke 22:41 says: **41** *He walked away, about a stone's throw, and knelt down and prayed,* **42** *"Father, if you are willing, please take this cup of suffering away from me. Yet I want your will to be done, not mine."*

Each author makes a point to illustrate this moment with similar perspectives. Jesus turned his eyes to the **Father** when he didn't know what else do to. These passages echo Jesus' current state of affairs and the suffering he felt. He needed power to carry on; a resolve that was much stronger than what he currently possessed, because the work of his flesh had him feeling *distressed*. The King of Kings was at the point of spiritual death and even begged for the circumstance to pass Him.

My personal resolve for you isn't to "just pray," your way through times that leave you feeling broken, however. Majority of the time, we feel unqualified to bring our issues to the Savior. My resolve is, that it is essential and imperative for you find a way to talk with the one who gave you life as if your life depended on it. Why? B*ecause* your indeed does depends you ability to communicate with your Father.

What's the proper way to pray, you ask? Let's turn to the Savior for our roadmap (remember, we are trying to model ourselves after the **man** that he was).

It is in the last cardinal Gospel of John where we see a much more intimate account of the life of Jesus as a whole. John is considered to be the beloved disciple–the one who was closest to Jesus during His ministry. If you recall, at the beginning of this journey we noted that Jesus took three individuals with Him as he walked further to pray: Peter, James, and John. These three could be considered Jesus' "day ones." John's testimony reveals a much more devoted moment during Jesus' despair. Let's take a look at how Jesus approaches the all-knowing Creator with his petition:

The Prayer of Jesus

John 17:1-26 (NLT)

1 *After saying all these things, Jesus looked up to heaven and*
said, "Father, the hour has come. Glorify your Son so he can give glory
back to you. ***2*** *For you have given him authority over everyone. He gives*
eternal life to each one you have given him. ***3*** *And this is the way to have*
eternal life–to know you, the only true God, and Jesus Christ, the one you
sent to earth. ***4*** *I brought glory to you here on earth by completing the*
work you gave me to do. ***5*** *Now, Father, bring me into the glory we shared*
before the world began.

6 *"I have revealed you to the ones you gave me from this world. They*
were always yours. You gave them to me, and they have kept your
word. ***7*** *Now they know that everything I have is a gift from you,* ***8*** *for I*
have passed on to them the message you gave me. They accepted it and
know that I came from you, and they believe you sent me.

9 "My prayer is not for the world, but for those you have given me,
because they belong to you. **10** All who are mine belong to you, and you
have given them to me, so they bring me glory. **11** Now I am departing
from the world; they are staying in this world, but I am coming to you.
Holy Father, you have given me your name; now protect them by the
power of your name so that they will be united just as we are. **12** During
my time here, I protected them by the power of the name you gave me. I
guarded them so that not one was lost, except the one headed for
destruction, as the Scriptures foretold.

13 "Now I am coming to you. I told them many things while I was with
them in this world so they would be filled with my joy. **14** I have given
them your word. And the world hates them because they do not belong
to the world, just as I do not belong to the world. **15** I'm not asking you to
take them out of the world, but to keep them safe from the evil
one. **16** They do not belong to this world any more than I do. **17** Make
them holy by your truth; teach them your word, which is truth. **18** Just as
you sent me into the world, I am sending them into the world. **19** And I
give myself as a holy sacrifice for them so they can be made holy by your
truth.

20 "I am praying not only for these disciples but also for all who will
ever believe in me through their message. **21**I pray that they will all be
one, just as you and I are one—as you are in me, Father, and I am in you.
And may they be in us so that the world will believe you sent me.

22 "I have given them the glory you gave me, so they may be one as
we are one. **23** I am in them and you are in me. May they experience such
perfect unity that the world will know that you sent me and that you love
them as much as you love me. **24** Father, I want these whom you have
given me to be with me where I am. Then they can see all the glory you
gave me because you loved me even before the world began!

25 "O righteous Father, the world doesn't know you, but I do; and
these disciples know you sent me. **26** I have revealed you to them, and I
will continue to do so. Then your love for me will be in them, and I will be
in them."

What a prayer to pray even in the face of surmounting (and literal) death. Yet, what a way to remain in gratitude for what God's purpose is, and what will come to past by following it. It is the assurance in God's promise that keeps Jesus at the throne of God's grace even in a season of loss (or death).

Here's the kicker...the Bible goes on to tell us in each of the four Gospels that Jesus didn't stop praying after his first prayer. It tells us that Jesus kept praying, **fervently**. Two more times to be exact. It also says that angels from heaven came down to strengthen Him while he was in prayer. It ALSO says that while he was praying–He was in such agony in the spirit–that his sweat fell to the ground like great drops of blood.

Jesus. Was. Pressed. Remember, the translation for Gethsemane is "oil-press." Ironic isn't it? An olive is able to produce something much more valuable when it's been pressed and squeezed. With the right pressure, what will you produce, and how valuable will your oil be?

So far, we've evaluated where Jesus was headed, the significance of His journey, and the emotional state of mind that Jesus had to be in during this time. I'd like to conclude this synopsis by looking at our last point–the men who were in Jesus' company during this prayer. The initial pilgrimage to Gethsemane involved all of the disciples that were at The Last Supper. Let's look at John 14:30-31 (NLT):

30 *"I don't have much more time to talk to you, because the ruler of this world approaches. He has no power over me,* ***31*** *but I will do what the Father requires of me, so that the world will know that I love the Father. Come, let's be going.*

Luke 22:39-40 (NLT) furthers the story: ***39*** *Then, accompanied by the disciples, Jesus left the upstairs room and went* ***as usual*** *to the Mount of Olives.* ***40*** *There he told them, "Pray that you will not give in to temptation."*

Mark 14:33-34 (NLT) goes on to show us the disciples Jesus took with him once at the place of prayer: ***33*** *He took Peter, James, and John with* *him, and he became deeply troubled and distressed.* **34** *He told them, "My soul is crushed with grief to the point of death. Stay here and keep watch with me."*

Why did Jesus do this? Was he playing favorites? Did he not want the other disciples to witness his anguish and suffering? I believe Jesus chose to bring a handful of individuals that He believed could support him spiritually. In a time of mental attack and physical distress, Jesus needed to make sure he had individuals in his environment who could intercede and believe on His behalf.

Your prayer life can't be a unilateral relationship between just you and the Father. The purpose of the entire faith walk is to reform the ***body*** of Christ, as a whole. And so, Jesus decides to bring some of the people closest to Him along for the journey. But watch what happens…

We now know that Jesus didn't pray just once. He prayed a total of three times during these last final moments of His life. But each time He returned from prayer, He found the people He thought He could count on asleep on the job. Let's read Mark 14:37-40 (NLT):

37 *Then he returned and found the disciples asleep. He said to Peter, "Simon, are you asleep? Couldn't you watch with me even one hour?* **38** *Keep watch and pray, so that you will not give in to temptation. For the spirit is willing, but the body is weak."*

39 *Then Jesus left them again and prayed the same prayer as before.* **40** *When he returned to them again, he found them sleeping, for they couldn't keep their eyes open. And they didn't know what to say.*

41 *When he returned to them the third time, he said, "Go ahead and sleep. Have your rest. But know–the time has come. The Son of Man is betrayed into the hands of sinners.* **42** *Up, let's be going. Look, my betrayer is here!"*

Jesus is facing death, sorrow, anxiety, and pain, and His best friends–the ones He should be able to depend on–are sleeping while He wrestles with his soul. They continue to fall asleep, up until the point where Jesus is captured. What happens when you're the only one who takes the vision God gave you seriously?

Everyone can't go where you are called to go. They may not be able to carry or manage the spiritual burden that comes with life pressing hard against you. Jesus found His most loyal supporters–His friends–unable and unwilling to be strong in the Spirit long enough to simply pray. "For the spirit is willing, but the body is weak," He said, hoping to petition His friends to stay (spiritually) alert. Yet, they were too focused on what their flesh needed during a time of crisis and left their Savior to fend for Himself. After all the times He was there for them, they couldn't stay up for an hour of prayer?

Prayer isn't always collective. It is intimate and refined in a way that brings you closer to God. While Jesus may have wanted to have His friends by His side, God may require us to be in a place where there are no bystanders, friends, or witnesses.

We opened this introduction with a verse from Philippians 4:6-7 (NLT). It reads: ***6*** *Don't worry about anything; instead, pray about everything. Tell God what you need, and thank Him for all He has done.* ***7*** *Then you will experience God's peace, which exceeds anything we can understand. His peace will guard your hearts and minds as you live in Christ Jesus.*

"As we live in Christ Jesus," speaks to the condition of our hearts and the strength of our faith as believers; our lives must be fully ***in*** Christ, believing in the work that He did, while modeling our lives after the love and faith He showed. This is how we obtain the peace we desperately keep searching for. When we are committed to fully living in Christ, then true transformation in our hearts and our minds can take place.

By cultivating a lifestyle that reflects that of the one Jesus taught about, we are then able to produce sustaining fruit from the good seeds we sow. Sow seeds of prayer and you will reap the grace of God in indescribable ways. Prayer is the secret sauce to our existence, and it is the secret sauce to living a divine, fruitful, and prosperous life.

With this book, it is my hope to provide you with 21 intentional prayers that cover whatever it is you hope to cultivate in your life. These prayers are intended to be read consecutively, more as daily prayers over the course of 21-days, but these can also be prayed, weekly, monthly, or whenever you feel the need to talk with God. It is my hope to not only provide the believer with an arsenal of anointed prayers, but to also give the ones still searching for eternal life a chance to learn the significance and power of prayer. It is my personal prayer that this journey helps inspire you to talk to God in a way that is unique and personal.

DAY 1: VISION

What is God speaking to you today about vision?

The Bible tells us that without a vision, people parish. Where there is no sight of where you intend on going, you end up lost in faith because you have no direction. Maybe the Lord is revealing to you today that your time is valuable. The vision God has for you exceeds someone's company, or place of employment. The only way the vision and plan of God can be actualized in your life is by staying anchored to His promises, for his ways are greater than ours. This allows you to be a free vessel who's available for God's true plan and purpose.

How can you apply God's vision into your day?

By allowing your life to be a witness to the glory of God's work. By seeing the bigger picture of God's manifestation of healing and love within your life and reciprocating that towards others. By focusing on the promises of God, and the blood His Son shed so that you could gain everything.

Your Prayer

God, you told me that if I believed in you, that I would have everlasting life. So today, I believe. I believe that you have predestined me to do greater works than what I currently see. Greater works that outweigh the status quo and normalcy around me. Greater works that break generational curses over my family. I believe you have birthed a billionaire inside of me; to produce works that not only change lives, but that also inspire your people for a better future. The vision I have for myself outweighs any words or thoughts that I could ever form or fathom. Your existence in my life gives me a vision of myself that has no earthly boundaries. I've seen the manifestation of your power and I want your favor to elevate me to a level that exists beyond my imagination, and beyond anything I can picture. There is no lack in you, and I belong to you, so I shall not lack.

In Jesus' name, Amen.

DAY 2: STRENGTH

EPHESIANS 6:10 | ISAIAH 40:29 | ISAIAH 40:31

What is God speaking to you today about strength?

Strength does not manifest as some supernatural ability to lift things beyond our human capabilities. True strength is what encourages you to keep going in as you reach and strive for your passion. The ability to sustain your faith through test and trials. Strength is the evidence of a faith that has been exercised and worked at over time. It is when you find yourself unsure of God's vision, that strength shows up to motivate you and encourage you to persevere towards the future (vision) He has prepared for us all.

How can you apply God's strength into your day?

It is my personal belief that the fore product of strength, is love. In love, there is *strength.* Why does God tell us to first *love* your enemy as you would yourself? Because the type of love required to do so cannot be found in yourself. There is strength in the blood of Jesus, because it was out of *love* He was sent to save us.

Your Prayer

It is my belief that love opens and unlocks doors that otherwise seem impossible to open. It is my prayer today, Lord, that I walk in pure love so that I can find strength in You. For in Your love, God, we can reach a spiritual depth where we find all of You. Help me reach a depth in you that connects others to your word. For in unconditional love, Your Spirit latches on to those who need an encounter from you. Through love my faith is activated. A renewal of Your Spirit brings a strength that not only encourages the me, but replenishes my faith and my *strength*. So today, we pray for your strength to show us what it means to love, for in love we find the fruit of the spirit. Your name is a strong tower, and the righteous run to you for protection and are safe.

We pray for all of these things, in Jesus' name, Amen.

DAY 3: PROVISION

PHILIPPIANS 4:19 | PSALMS 34:10 | MATTHEW 6:28

What is God speaking to you today about provision?

The provision of God can come in any form, at any time, from anyone. Provision does not always mean monetary substance. Provision often times is essentially God making a way, even when it feels like there isn't one in a particular season of your life.

How can you apply God's provision into your day?

Be willing to accept that God will always be your provider, and that His provision covers *everything*. Our trust in Him is the very thing that activates His spirit of provision. He tells us that the birds do not store their food, for they know that their Creator will bring more tomorrow. Harboring what you have and own out of fear of being without, only proves that you do not believe that God is capable of providing for you.

Your Prayer

Even young lions become tired and hungry. But, the difference between myself and the lion is that, I am connected to a source that never depletes. My trust in the Lord unlocks every gift that I have inside of me. I turn to You, Oh Lord, for nourishment and rest rather than relying on the conditions and vises of the world to make me whole. Since I trust You, then I must know that there is DAILY sustainability for my soul that will forever replenish. So, just like the birds of the sky, I will trust in my Father to feed and soothe the needs of his children. Today, I put my faith and my trust in You fully, allowing you to be my way-maker.

I pray these things be added unto me, In the name of Jesus, Amen.

DAY 4: GOD'S WILL

MATTHEW 6:10 | EPHESIANS 5:17 | PROVERBS 19:21

What is God speaking to you today about His will?

God's plan will always prevail and His truth judges all things in their due season. The personal thoughts you have from time to time may seem misplaced or out of left field, but God always has a plan for what occurs in your life. Once you surrender your entire being to the full scope of His grace, those misplaced thoughts and emotions become fuel to achieve what God has planned for you. Weeping may endure for a night, but there is always joy available to us the next morning. Your joy can be placed in the known fact that He will ALWAYS see you through; if you're aligned in Him fully.

How can you apply the Will of God into your day?

Sometimes, I think it is really easy to follow the routines of life as they unfold. Things become so redundant, that we easily get to the point where we make plans for our future that do not include God. Our compliance makes us anxious, because we aren't where we want to be. But our life circumstances and temptations should be counted as opportunities for great joy, for we know that the challenges we face are only opportunities for God to show up and blow our minds.

Your Prayer

God, Your plans for me, only You know. It is my prayer that the plans you have for me exceed my wildest dreams and surpass my reality. I truly pray and ask you to keep my mind focused on the fact that my day to day may stay the same, but your plans for me are always at work, regardless how complacent I may feel. Continue to refresh my mind with Your word, that explicitly tells me that the plans You have for me consist of prosperity and abundance. Your plans never include defeat or brokenness, even when the plans I make for myself leave me this way. Your will was done two thousand years ago, despite the plans that men had for Your son's life. Teach me and help me follow your voice at all times so that my plans may prosper according to Your will.

These things I pray in the name of Jesus, Amen.

DAY 5: PURPOSE

PROVERBS 19:21 | PSALMS 33:11

What is God speaking to you today about purpose?

By leaning on the Will of God, your soul is led to purpose; for purpose is the reason for which something is done or created, or for which something exists. Place yourself in Him fully and you gain access to the true destiny of your existence. Yet, your mental state must represent a commitment to carrying out a dedication to him fully. This is what we call intention. Be intentional about your love for others, and your ways of peace, and God's purpose for your life has no choice but to manifest.

How can you apply God's purpose into your day?

Purpose reveals everything. Following the Will of God unleashes revelations that blow your mind. Remind yourself that God's purpose and will work hand in hand. His will gives you purpose and with that comes everything you need. So keep your mind–your intentions– on His ways of truth and faith and watch your destiny fall into place.

Your Prayer

O Lord, you have examined my heart and know everything there is to know about me. God, you know when I sit down and stand up. You know my thoughts even when I'm far away from your presence, which lets me know that I can never escape from your Spirit. You made all the delicate, inner parts of my body and perfectly knitted me together while I was in my mother's womb. Thank you for making me so wonderfully complex! Your workmanship is marvelous! You saw me before I was born. Every day of my life was recorded in Your book of promise. Every moment of my existence was laid out before a single day had passed. Search me, O, God and know my heart; test me and know my anxious thoughts. Point out anything in me that offends you, and lead me along the path of everlasting life.

These things I pray in Your Son's name, Amen.

DAY 6: WISDOM

JAMES 1:5 | PROVERBS 2:6 | PROVERBS 16:16

What is God speaking to you today about wisdom?

Take a moment to sit and meditate on what God may be saying to you. Search the Holy Spirit for your own revelation. Be intentional as you search your heart for His voice.

How can you apply the wisdom of God into your day?

God's unfailing access to whatever you need allows you to approach the throne for wisdom whenever you need it. Its abundance is readily available. Your daily struggle with guidance allows you to call on Him to provide you with a new sense of direction. The quality of having experience, knowledge, and good judgment sometimes fails us, so calling on our Father for a wisdom that encompasses the things we have no clue about, is by far one of the greatest advantages we could have.

Your Prayer

Lord God, when I feel lost help me remember that Your divine wisdom can clear up any situation that I am struggling with. Asking for Your wisdom comes with no consequence, which increases the confidence that I have in coming to the throne for Your guidance. God, even in this moment, I ask for You to reveal the meaning and depth of Your wisdom. I desire to explore what comes with walking with You in pure wisdom, being 100% guided by Your ways. Today, I move my pride, my agenda, and my self out of the way so You can move in my life like never before.

In Jesus' name I pray, Amen.

DAY 7: DIRECTION AND DISCERNMENT

PSALMS 32:8 | JOHN 16:13 | PSALMS 119:125

What is God speaking to you today about direction and discernment?

His direction may come in ways that are unconventional and strange, but once His direction has been revealed, it makes sense in the instant it's given. He's reminding and reiterating to you today, that you truly have a divine connection like no other when concerning spiritual discernment, because your spirit is of Him.

How can you apply direction and discernment into your day?

By remembering that God will continue to guide you on the best pathway for your life. The Holy Spirit is the advisor that brings truth to you directly from the Father and Son seated in heaven. Through discernment, we begin to understand God's laws and ways, but never fully. Be open to allowing the direction of the spirit of truth to guide you using discernment.

Your Prayer

God, it is my prayer that you allow me to never miss the Holy Spirit's direction when it speaks. Its guidance for my life is in all truth, and in truth I prosper. Allow me to remember that there is no path that I take that you haven't already prepared me for. Continue to fine tune my spiritual ears to hear your voice clearly. Allow me to heed your direction for the sake of saving your people. I want to only hear from you. Remove the clutter from my mind so that your voice can engulf my life. I want to be available for complete guidance and obedience. Advise me and watch over me so the I can complete your will for not only my life, but also for the people of God I am supposed to save.

I pray for these things in the name of Jesus Christ, Amen.

DAY 8: STEWARDSHIP

COLOSSIANS 3:23-24 | 1 PETER 4:10 | PROVERBS 21:20

What is God speaking to you today about stewardship?

People of God need someone to manage, assess, and organize their gifts for the sake of the kingdom. These gifts being property, resources for funding, land and other earthly possessions. Your personal provision over the people of God will reveal and extract gifts that will save the kingdom. Who's fighting for their roommates soul? A grandparent's? A mother's? There must be someone who can amass the resources necessary; supervising over the gifts of the kingdom and serving others in their work.

How can you apply stewardship into your day?

The gifts God has already bestowed on us should be used to bless others and to bring them closer to Him. By allowing yourself the ability to use the gifts you innately have to assist others, your faithfulness in serving the body helps the whole rather than just yourself. God rewards those who are selfless.

Your Prayer

God, it is my prayer today that you reveal more to me about what it means to serve not only You, but the people in Your kingdom. I pray that You will continue to raise me to be an organizer of resources, who can amass the souls of Christ for your glory. My service to You is my obedience, and I ask you to make me a good steward and guardian over everything that I touch, see and encounter. But, You must equip me with Your wisdom and Your grace in order for me to give the people what they desire from you.

I pray for these things in the name of Jesus Christ, Amen.

DAY 9: FRUITS OF THE SPIRIT

GALATIANS 5:22-23

What is God speaking to you today about the fruits of the spirit?

There is nothing that we cannot obtain when we have access to the Holy Spirit or, the Spirit of truth. In Him, every good thing exists which means we have immediate access to qualities of love, joy, peace, patience, kindness, goodness faithfulness, gentleness, and self-control.

How can you apply the fruit of the spirit into your day?

God's essence is complete in the Holy Spirit by the fruit that it produces; fruit which we have total access to, making it readily available to us at this very second. When you need peace, if you are in the Holy Spirit, peace is immediately made available to you. If you need self-control for your attitude, it exist in abundance in the Holy Spirit, which means you have access to it. Jesus told His disciples that the flesh was weak, but the spirit is willing...He meant that when your flesh can't find the support it needs to carry on, the spirit will make way for things that your physical body can not.

Your Prayer

It is my prayer today that Your fruit continues to hang low enough for me to reach it. God, never do I want to doubt what I have access to. Between Your Son dying for my sins, and sending the Holy Spirit to make us whole, I know there's nothing more powerful than a child of God who bears the fruit of the Holy Spirit. There is nothing lacking in You. I pray that when I can call on the fruits of Your Spirit, that your presence shows up immediately to change my circumstance. I ask that your fruit stay fresh and implanted on my heart, as I carry out the will of God here on this earth.

In Jesus' name, Amen.

DAY 10: PURITY

PSALMS 51:1-13 | PROVERBS 16:2 | PHILIPPIANS 2:3

What is God speaking to you today about purity?

Purity is a constant examination of the heart; a daily confession of how much we need the Lord to keep us clean and refreshed. The Lord knows the conditions of the heart of His people, so it's my believe that if we walk in the purity of Christ and his love, then our heart have no choice but to be fully submitted to Him.

How can you apply God's purity into your day?

By practicing a humbleness that lift others up with humility and unconditional love. By submitting your works to God rather than trying to fulfill the plans you have for yourself. With the trust that you are building in Him, the plans that you have will have no choice but to prosper under His guidance.

Your Prayer

God, I may not do everything the way I'm supposed to do it, nor do I do it as soon as You tell me to, but it is my hope that You wash me clean every day. I recognize the sin that I carry daily, and I repent for what weaknesses I have. But today God, I ask You to make me new. Keep me pure so that Your anointing can shine, even when my sin tries to stop your glory from making me whole. Continue to work on the condition of my heart so that those who need from me, can receive everything I am supposed to offer. I believe that when you see my heart, you see love and purity and a *new* creature. It is my faith that assures me that you see my intentions as just and holy because I am a reflection of You.

In Jesus' name I pray, Amen.

DAY 11: LOVE

1 JOHN 4:7 | CORINTHIANS 13:4-8 | EPHESIANS 4:2

What is God speaking to you today about love?

Love is one of my favorite qualities and gifting in the Spirit because love always wins. God is the full manifestation of love. The gift of His Son was the example of perfect love given to filthy people who didn't deserve such a gift. To cherish something so valuable as your very own offspring's life, yet willingly kill it to see others saved...sounds like real love to me.

How can you apply the love of God into your day?

The key to love, and that unconditionally, is patience. Ephesians 4:2 to tell us to make allowances for all our brothers and sisters because of the love we have for them. Walking by the grace of God's love allows you to connect directly with God the Father, because he sent his son out of pure, unadulterated, perfect love for just for you.

Your Prayer

Lord God, the love You show me daily can never be matched by anything that I can physically do or say. So God, it is my prayer that the unconditional love I show your children, be a sacrifice that is a reflection of the love you showed me the day Your Son died. God, allow me to sit at the throne of love forever. Prepare my heart to be a house of love that always has room for your people. I pray that my practice of unconditional love becomes my assignment daily, because You are a loving God. Let my words be blessed because of the love that overflows from me. Let bitterness and hatred flee from me, as I practice loving others the way you love me.

In Your name I pray, Amen.

DAY 12: FAITHFULNESS

PSALMS 119:11 | 1 KINGS 2:3-4 | HEBREWS 10:23

What is God speaking to you today about faithfulness?

His consistency in being the Lord of your life should give you the encouragement to walk in the trust you have in Him, so that you can succeed in everything you do. But, being consistent and faithful by following His word and commitments every day, is the predicate for unlimited grace and prosperity to flow in your life.

How can you apply God's faithfulness into your day?

By remaining confident in Him. By carrying out the obedience of the Lord, your God. By trusting your salvation in the living Christ and walking in the authority of the Word of God. Hold onto the confession of your hope without wavering, for He promised to be faithful to the words that He has spoken over you life while you were yet being formed.

Your Prayer

Father, as I grow in You and become more vulnerable in Your presence, continue to remind me that in the faithfulness to the instructions of Your way, there is unlimited power. Being consistently reliant on you gives me power to not only find peace, but to find purpose and truth. I have only you to lead my thoughts and ambitions. Everlasting God, I set my hope on You, for you tell me that the Word will never return unto you void or incomplete. Continue to strengthen my mind to never waiver from the plans that you have already started implementing before I could even breathe. I will trust you with everything I have.

In the name of Jesus, I pray, Amen.

DAY 13: WHOLENESS

3 JOHN 1:2 | 1 PETER 2:24 | ISAIAH 53:5

What is God speaking to you today about wholeness?

Jesus died so that you could have complete immunity from death and sin. He took care of everything so that you could have *everything*. His sacrifice on the cross was the gate to the wholeness you have in him, making you spiritually invincible.

How can you apply the wholeness of God into your day?

By remembering that not only did Jesus pay it all for you, but also remembering that in the wholeness that you have, there is freedom in every aspect and area of your entire existence. The faith to believe Him for the finished work is the key to unlocking his riches in glory while down here on earth.

Your Prayer

Heavenly Father, today I pray that You remind me that I am made whole in You. When everything around me feels incomplete or damaged, please teach my heart that the saving grace You released on Calvary is all I need to sustain me. Your blood redeemed me forever, and in redemption, there is power to conquer anything I could possibly imagine. I pray that You continue to strengthen my faith in what you've already finished for my life. Let me listen only to you and the voice that cries out for salvation. Create in me a clean heart and renew a right spirit within me.

These things I ask in Your name, Amen.

DAY 14: SPIRITUAL GROWTH

3 JOHN 1:2 | 1 PETER 2:24 | ISAIAH 53:5

What is God speaking to you today about spiritual growth?

The key to spiritual success and growth is the simple notion of consistency and commitment. When you become a part of God, you live in His essence. That essence is extended into the fiber of your being, allowing you to access a side of God that only comes by being faithful to His way.

How can you apply spiritual growth into your day?

By remembering to follow what you know about Him. This is the truth and your faith grows strong in the truth. As you spend more time in Him and with Him and His ways, you begin to see the manifestation of the fruit of the spirit like peace and love. Your life must be built on him.

Your Prayer

God, it is my prayer that my growth in you never gets stunted. It is my hope that today I will become the biggest thing this world has seen in order to give you glory. God, my prayer is that that your word becomes so implanted in me that I won't to be able to turn away from your truth. Let this spiritual growth become a genetic fusion; a fusion into my very existence so that I can't rid myself of it. God, this spiritual growth I am walking into must be sustained. There are so many things I must get done with You and I do not want to waste another second. Please don't leave me behind. Forgive me when I miss the mark. I am growing.

I pray these things in Your Son's name, Amen.

DAY 15: RELATIONSHIPS, COMMUNITY & UNITY

EPHESIANS 4:2-3 | 1 CORINTHIANS 1:10

What is God speaking to you today about relationships, community, and unity?

Your heart has to be built on relationships, community, and unity. Your desire has to be one that focuses on the world being united together, all colors and creeds, under one truth, serving one God. You've been called for such a purpose in Him. Your job is to mend people; to mend souls.

How can you apply relationships, community and unity into your day?

By showing up in peace, offering love and generosity to your fellow brothers and sisters, our spiritual (yet, earthly) siblings are all on different ranges of spiritual awareness and the journey will take time. But providing them these allowances proves your love and activates patience. There is one body, and we are all united in spirit.

Your Prayer

God, strengthen me so I can strengthen others. My earnest desire is to see people find the Christ that I've found. In ways indescribable, I've tapped into the well of life that has replenished my entire being. I believe the wealth of life is a heavenly place, a place where I can go to find continued renewal of my strength, love, compassion and anointing. God, allow me to pull from this well, and I ask that you never let it run dry so that I can lead many people to Your promise. Strengthen the body so that Your purpose can be revealed.

In Your name I pray, Amen.

DAY 16: FAVOR

EPHESIANS 4:2-3 | 1 CORINTHIANS 1:10

What is God speaking to you today about His favor?

Favor is a direct result of obedience and sacrifice. Favor is unlocked and accessible when we decide to obey God's word and stay faithful in the commandments of the Lord. Keeping his virtual and she planted in our daily existence is the only way to obtain favor from God.

How can you apply God's favor into your day?

By keeping your mind and thoughts concerning God and man focused on His promise. He blesses the godly and surrounds them in His love, so if my intentions reflect the qualities of God, then the blessings have no choice but to take care of all my needs, or in other words, favor.

Your Prayer

God, I pray and ask you to remember my obedience and sacrifice to protecting and living out your word. In keeping my hope on you, it's my prayer that your favor grows exponentially. God, I pray for endless and unwavering favor that makes the devil mad as hell. My prayer is that your goodness over-saturates my life. I want your favor to not only touch my life, but to saturate the lives of those around me. See my trust as dedication to the goodness that you outlined in your word and encouraged me to follow. In trusting in you, you told me that all things would be made new.

In Jesus name I pray, Amen.

DAY 17: YOUR CITY

JEREMIAH 29:7 | MATTHEW 6:10 | 2 CHRONICLES 7:14

What is God speaking to you today your city?

God's hope is to restore the land where his children reside in order to carry out the will of God. He wants us to work for peace and prosperity so the land's welfare can thrive for the good of all people.

How can you apply God's view of your city into your day?

In your efforts to build a better future for yourself and a stronger relationship with Christ, your work for peace and harmony shouldn't be just for the well-being of believers and lost souls, but for the entire city you live in. As believers, it's important that we allow our (God's) spirit to saturate the streets with his presence to see change in the heart of the people we encounter daily.

Your Prayer

God, give me the strength and the courage to fight not just the flesh, but the powers and principalities of my city. I know that when standing in Your grace and favor that all things will work together for my good. I pray for potency and a level of legitimacy in the spirit that causes men to bow and submit to the authority of the Christ that is in me. No demon in hell can conquer the anointing that I carry, and as I begin to elevate in your truth, I ask that you prepare me to be able to articulate your words of love and prosperity in an effective way that changes hearts. Let me be wise with words for the sake of your coming Kingdom.

In Jesus' name, Amen.

DAY 18: MIRACLES

MATTHEW 19:26 | JOB 5:8-9 | EPHESIANS 3:20-21

What is God speaking to you today about miracles?

With Him all things are possible, and nothing is ever too complicated of a task for my God. Job teaches us to go to God and make a case, for He does great things too marvelous to understand. Miracles occur around us every day, but the misalignment of our spirit blinds us from seeing the work that is actually being done. They are not exclusive to detrimental circumstances. Simply asking Him for help is the miracle.

How can you apply the miracles of God into your day?

By staying confident in God's accessibility that grants me everlasting mercy and justice in Him. I truly lack nothing, for I am in Him, and in Him miracles are an every day blessing and gift I can call on.

Your Prayer

God, my prayer is that You instill in me a pure heart that worships Your presence daily. By staying in worship and in spirit I am walking according to your laws; which activates your glory in support of all that I do. The miracle of your word is that with You, everything is possible. Nothing is ever impossible. Your mighty work within me grants me the ability to do things I wouldn't be able to do if not for You. Keep me humbled in Your presence so that You always come first in my life forever. With you first, my world is endless and opportunities abound.

These things I pray in Your name, Amen.

DAY 19: LEADERSHIP

1 KINGS 3:9 | 1 CORINTHIANS 15:58 | PSALMS 91

What is God speaking to you today about leadership?

Leaders must call upon the strength of God in order to be effective. Jeremiah tells us that by ourselves we cannot govern the people of the Lord. Choose to be in Him at all times so that way we may gain everything we need to be effective servants.

How can you apply the grace for leaders into your day?

By hiding in God always, for He's the only truth and life. For you, His faithful promises are your protection and your place of safety.

Your Prayer

Dad, as you raise me to be your effective leader of truth and prosperity, keep me covered in you. Rejuvenate my body with your protection and camp your angels around me. Teach me wisdom so that can make sound decisions that only forward the plan you have for me.

In Jesus' name, Amen.

DAY 20: OTHERS (THE LOST & FOUND)

ACTS 16:31 | COLOSSIANS 4:3 | COLOSSIANS 2:6-7 | COLOSSIANS 1:9-10

What is God speaking to you today about the lost & found?

Every believer has found themselves either lost or found at some given point when walking with Christ. It is inevitable when following the will of God that is much bigger than fleshly desires that you sometimes lose your way. When found, it is the responsibility of a servant to testify about the goodness, and proudly encourage others about what God can do.

How can you apply grace for the lost and found into your day?

The theme for the past few days of prayer has been that the direction of the Lord is perfect. Your strength in witnessing to others displays your diligence in carrying out your dedication to Christ.

Your Prayer

Dear God, allow me to remember that there was a point in my life where You didn't exist the way You should have. In my obedience to go to a secret place to find Your destiny for me, I found love, healing and splendor. I was lost, with no hope of what my future could look like. I now ask You to instill courage and boldness in me to witness to those who are lost like I was. Let me thrive on the revealing mysteries of your faith that I share with others. Provide me with healing words to touch someone deep inside their broken soul; to encourage them to keep pressing forward, for the reward will be so great. I will not be afraid, because our God truly wants the best for us.

In the mighty name of Jesus I pray, Amen.

DAY 21: REVIVAL

PSALMS 85:6 | ISAIAH 57:15

What is God speaking to you today about revival?

God is the only being who can give you one touch that can revive every dead place. Such an encounter conditions a rejoicing in Him for his continued goodness and mercy that renews everyday. But revival is also about the souls that still need Him.

How can you apply the revival of God's word into your day?

God tells me that He dwells in high and holy places, but also dwells with the humble and contrite. This is so He can learn and understand how to heal those in need. In faith and spiritual maturity, revival is no respecter of persons, and in order to be effective you must know how to dwell in any circumstance to be as effective as God needs you to be.

Your Prayer

Here is your chance to practice a your own prayer. Focus on what you need from God and allow the Holy Spirit to direct you to truth. Focus on His grace and love with intention. Talk to your Father about the revival of your life and what you want it to look like. Remember we believe for all of these things in the name of His Son that died for us to be made whole.

Amen.

Made in the USA
Monee, IL
06 April 2021

64046664R00038